Careers For
Computer
Buffs

Interviews by Andrew Kaplan

Photographs by Eddward Keating and Carrie Boretz

CHOICES
The Millbrook Press
Brookfield, Connecticut

Produced in association with Agincourt Press.

Photographs by Edward Keating, except: Cheryl Chambers
(David B. Sutton), Susan G. McBride (Jim Gensheimer), Peter
McClard (Carrie Boretz), Wendy Perez (Carrie Boretz), Walter Prue
(Jim Gensheimer), Don Small (Orensel Brumfield).

Cataloging-in-Publication Data

Kaplan, Andrew.
Careers for computer buffs/interviews by Andrew Kaplan,
photographs by Edward Keating and Carrie Boretz.

64 p.; ill.: (Choices)
Bibliography: p.
Includes index.

Summary: Interviews with fourteen people who work in careers of
interest to young people who like computers.
1. Computer applications.   2. Computer engineering.
3. Computer scientists.   4. Computer software.
I. Keating, Edward, ill.   II. Boretz, Carrie, ill.
III. Title.   IV. Series.
1991   004.6 KAP
ISBN 1-56294-021-X

Contents

Introduction

In this book, 14 people who work in computer-related fields talk about their careers — what their work involves, how they got started, and what they like (and dislike) about it. They tell you things you should know before beginning a computer-related career and show you how feeling comfortable with computers can lead to many different types of jobs.

Many computer-related jobs are found in the sciences, such as physics, aeronautics, and engineering. But just as many can be found in fields that use computers much less formally. Video game designers and computer musicians, for instance, use computers for entertainment, while computer-aided designers use them to help draft plans and blueprints. You don't have to know much computer science to market your own software programs, but you do have to have a feel for how the machines work.

The 14 careers described here are just the beginning, so don't limit your sights. At the end of this book, you'll find short descriptions of a dozen more careers you may want to explore, as well as suggestions on how to get more information. Computers are everywhere in the business world. If you're a computer buff, you'll find a wide range of career choices open to you.

Joan B. Storey, M.B.A., M.S.W.
Series Career Consultant

"I got my first computer
when I was 15."

GEOFF ENGELSTEIN

COMPUTER-AIDED DESIGNER

Scotch Plains, New Jersey

WHAT I DO:

I work for a company that does consulting work for plastics design. Basically, we design plastic parts for various consumer and medical products such as air conditioner covers, towel dispensers, and cosmetic cases. People come to us with projects that are in various stages: They may have something that's sketched on a napkin, or a part that already exists but has given them trouble. We take a look at it, talk to them about how they want that part to perform, and then come up with a design that fulfills their requirements.

As director of computer-aided design (CAD), I perform two basic functions: design and analysis. When I design, I use the computer to create a three-dimensional drawing of the part. The computer allows me to see every aspect of the finished part: how it will look from every possible perspective, what its texture will be, and how it will fit together.

Then, once the part is designed, I use the computer to analyze how it will perform. For example, I'll figure out how a bookshelf may react to various stresses. That way, I can tell whether it will be strong enough for the use that's intended. Or a cosmetics manufacturer may come to me with a compact case that has a tiny discoloration on top caused by the manufacturing process. To locate the problem, I'll use the computer to analyze what happens when the plastic fills the product mold. Then I try to identify the error that creates the discoloration and figure out a cost-effective way to correct the problem.

Geoff inspects a part that he has designed.

HOW I GOT STARTED:
I got my first computer when I was 15. I used it all through high school, and did things like design games. Although I didn't study computers in college — I studied physics instead — I was still learning about them and using them as tools in my work. I had the attitude then that I still have now: The computer itself isn't something to spend all your time on, but it is a useful tool for work on other things.

After I got my physics degree, I came to work for a different part of the company than I'm in now. At that time, I worked on inertial naviga-tional systems for aircraft — little black boxes that tell pilots where they are, how fast they're going, and the direction in which they're headed. After a year and a half, I moved into electronics design work. Then the plastics division of the company bought a lot of computers, and they began looking for someone with a computer background who could learn computer-aided design. I transferred to that division.

HOW I FEEL ABOUT IT:
What's nice about the work is that every job is different, and it's not just rote work. When each project comes in,

Geoff consults with a colleague on a new design.

Geoff must make a detailed set of drawings for each part.

Although there's no creative thinking involved, you have to be very careful. You've got to lay out all the dimensions, and check the drawings to make sure that everything is accurate, complete, and understandable. Because you have to go over the drawings three or four times, it can get a little tedious.

WHAT YOU SHOULD KNOW:
The most common background for this kind of work is mechanical engineering. But any kind of a scientific or engineering background is sufficient if you also have an open mind. The most important quality a designer can have is a willingness to think about why things are made the way they are, how they fit together, and what makes them work.

As for the computer aspect of the job, you don't need to know computer-aided design before you start. You just need to be comfortable with computers. Training courses can teach you CAD. Just about every company that has a CAD section sends their designers out for training or has some sort of an in-house CAD training program.

The hours are pretty standard, unless there's a deadline coming up. The pay is good. Salaries for designers start around $25,000 and run into the $50,000 range.

you really have to think about it. You have to look at it intelligently, analyze it, identify the problems, and come up with imaginative ways to overcome them.

The one part of this work that isn't very interesting, however, is making the drawings. Once you've designed a part, and it's working, you've got to come up with a set of detailed drawings for it. These drawings have to be exact enough for somebody in Hong Kong to make the product mold from them.

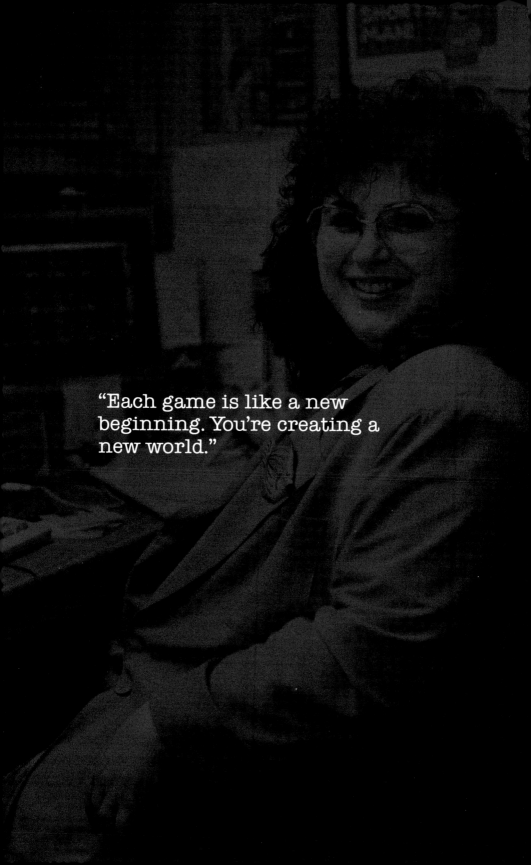

"Each game is like a new beginning. You're creating a new world."

SUSAN G. McBRIDE

VIDEO GAME DESIGNER

San Jose, California

WHAT I DO:

I come up with ideas for home computer video games, figure out how they would be played, and determine their basic graphic look. Then, I work with a team to fill out these designs. Right now my team includes another animator and a programmer, but we also get help from graphics, audio, and software support personnel. When I used to work on coin-operated arcade games, I worked on teams with two or three other programmers and up to five animators.

After getting an idea for a game, you produce story boards and thumbnail sketches that show how the new game will look. Then, once the concept is approved, you work out all the characters and the opponents, what the moment-to-moment ac-

Susan designs video games that are played on home computers.

tion will be like, and how the controls will work. This stage includes producing working graphics and a model of the controls. When all that's finished, the concept is reviewed again and focus groups are held to estimate consumer reaction. Finally, the game is field tested.

Home games are different from coin-operated games. In coin-op games, you're trying to entice people to put their quarters into a machine. You know they're not going to play for long. But with home games, people own the cartridges, so you know they'll want to play the games for a long time. As a result, home games need to be more exploratory and graphically exciting. They're better suited to adventure formats than coin-op games.

HOW I GOT STARTED:

I came to this work by way of drawing. When I was a kid, I

Susan and a colleague make plans for a new game.

was always drawing. I drew my own comic books and illustrated T-shirts. In college, I almost double majored in graphic design and science. But I realized that what I really liked the most about biology was drawing the animals we worked with. So I decided to major exclusively in graphic design.

Graphic design led me in turn to animation and film. A film teacher of mine recommended me to Atari for a position involving computer graphics. He knew about the little characters I liked to animate and about an award-winning film that I made called *Mangia, Mangia, Mangia.* Done before Pac Man, it was about a little space creature that went around gobbling things up. I guess that my professor —

and Atari — thought the film proved I was a natural for creating video games and characters.

HOW I FEEL ABOUT IT:
What I really like about working in the game industry is the chance to be creative and to come up with concepts that provide fun and entertainment for people. The games take people away from the world for a little while.

Each game is like a new beginning. You're creating a new world, and it's a thrill when it comes together. When you come up with an idea you love, you suddenly know it's going to be a hit, and that's very exciting.

WHAT YOU SHOULD KNOW:
There are a number of different routes into this business.

You can come in as a programmer or, as I did, through animation. But even if your route is animation, you still need to get as much of a background in computers as you can.

To break in, you need to have a degree. Animators need to have a strong film background with a degree in something like film, animation, or art. Programmers need computer degrees. And after you're in, it's still a good idea to keep learning. Game designers need to have as much computer knowledge as they can. For example, although I'm already established in the industry, I'm getting additional software background and working toward a master's degree.

The pay varies. A beginning animator might make around $30,000, while a game designer can make $85,000. Some people get royalties, which can double or triple their salaries. Another way to go is to open up your own house. Get an animator, a designer, a programmer, an engineer, and an audio person. Then develop games, sell them to companies, and get royalties. This arrangement offers you the potential to earn a lot of money.

To create these games, you need to enjoy children's culture and know what's going on with kids. Obviously, it helps to know what kids like to watch and the music they like to listen to. I go to science fiction conventions, arcades, and movies to keep up, and I also buy comic books and kids' magazines.

Susan tries out a video game she has designed.

"Music theory opened my mind."

PETER McCLARD

COMPUTER MUSICIAN

New York, New York

WHAT I DO:
I play computer music, and I also develop software that other people can use to play computer music. The goal that my partner and I have set for ourselves is to produce software that anyone can use to create music that is complex, beautiful, and new. Our performance-related software is different from standard music software, which deals with such labor-saving functions as scoring music, recording music, and running synthesizers.

We have two products out right now and several more on the way. The one that's most widely known is called Pixound. It enables you to take any graphic image, whether it's a Van Gogh painting or a photo of a friend, and translate that image into music. What

Peter's software allows him to play music on the computer.

you're actually doing is both creating music and exploring the structure of the picture.

You put the image on a computer screen. Then you "play" the image by pointing to different parts of the picture. The program assigns chords to each hue and shape in the picture, and as you point, the synthesizer plays music. The brighter colors sound lighter and higher, and the darker colors sound lower and more subdued. Because you can take different paths through the graphic, pause at different times, and point in different rhythms, each painting has an infinite number of musical possibilities. There are also various adjustments you can make to "tune" a painting.

HOW I GOT STARTED:
My involvement with music started at the age of 8, when I got my own guitar. By the time I was 15, I was playing

Peter translates a picture into music.

all kinds of music, including classical and rock. In college, I studied a lot of music and music theory.

Music theory opened my mind and led to my first ideas about computer music. As I studied theory, I began to think about the origin, evolution, and structure of music. I also started to see how computers could expand the boundaries of music. I got interested in the mathematical structures of tonality and music, and how computers could work with these structures.

After college, I played in different bands for a couple of years, and I also got my own computer and played with that. Eventually, I developed a program called

Hyperchord and played a concert with it. Then I moved from Santa Fe, where I'd been living, to New York.

During my first year here, the Hyperchord software was still just for my personal use. However, as people heard my stuff, they encouraged me to take it further and look into its commercial possibilities. Once I hooked up with my partner, the software began to develop at a faster rate.

A big turning point came during Christmas of 1989 when I went home to visit my family. They showed a lot of interest in my software, and my brother-in-law, who has worked at I.B.M. and been president of a supercomputer company, thought the program had great potential.

Soon after that, my family invested money in my work and formed a corporation to market the programs in a more intense way. Now we're getting responses to my software from a wide variety of people including musicians, artists, music and art therapists, and academic types.

HOW I FEEL ABOUT IT:

Developing and working with this software is great. I'm into the music, and it's fun working with computers. But in addition to that, I really like demonstrating the software. These programs attract interesting people and provoke fascinating questions. It's exciting for me to be able to share a unique musical experience with people, and to see how they respond to it. I love it when people who've never used a computer come in, sit down with the program, and get into it.

WHAT YOU SHOULD KNOW:

I think you're going to see great expansion in the field of computer music. One of the things the computer does is help you transcend the physical limitations of the body. When you work with a computer, you can bring almost any idea in your mind to life. In fact, the computer becomes a sort of amplifier for the mind.

That's a powerful thing, and I think that, as computers become easier and cheaper to use, they will be something people will have a hard time resisting.

Peter uses musical instruments to create programs.

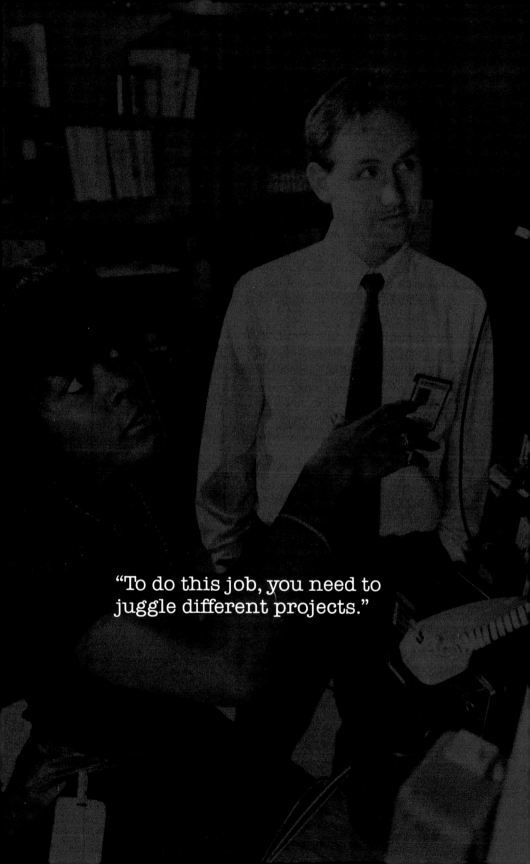

"To do this job, you need to juggle different projects."

CHERYL CHAMBERS

COMMUNICATIONS ENGINEER

Naperville, Illinois

WHAT I DO:

I'm a member of the technical staff here at Bell Laboratories, and I work with telecommunications circuitry. Specifically, I write software for a circuit board that handles digital phone calls. My program allows the board to tell which digits are being dialed when customers use their phones. Right now, we're trying to increase the number of calls that the board can handle.

Projects go through different phases. Currently, I'm at the front end of a project, which means that I attend a lot of meetings. At these meetings, each of us talks about the aspect of the project for which we're responsible. We discuss how far the planning for each component has progressed, and then we look at the over-

all design. We have to make sure that all the components will interface, or work together well.

The next phase of the project will be the design phase, during which I will write the software that goes with the circuit board. On this particular project, the software is very complex, so rather than working on it alone, I'm a team leader for a group of six people. I hope to be able to break the software down into distinct pieces so that each person on my team can do a different job. After the design phase, there's a lot of testing before the product is put into use. The typical time frame for a project of this size, from beginning to end, is one year.

HOW I GOT STARTED:

While I was in high school, I really began to enjoy my science and math courses. I also attended various summer

Cheryl makes sure that the phone system runs smoothly.

19

Cheryl writes software for circuit boards like this one.

programs. One, which was at Bell Labs, was a three-week program during which students got to see what engineers did on a day-to-day basis. Another, which was at the University of Notre Dame, gave high school students a chance to interact with Notre Dame's engineering faculty as well as engineers from various corporations. As a result of these programs, I became interested in engineering, and went to Notre Dame.

When I was at Notre Dame, I majored in electrical engineering and worked during the summer at Bell Labs. Then, at the end of my junior year, I applied for and received a fellowship, which

provided me with a summer job following my graduation and also paid for my graduate studies. After I earned a master's degree in electrical engineering, I came here to Bell Labs.

HOW I FEEL ABOUT IT:
What I like most about my job is the variety. I don't just sit at my terminal and write software all day. What I do depends on what phase of the project we're in and can include planning, writing documentation, writing the actual software, working with the hardware, and testing the system. At any given moment, I may be in touch with many different facets of the project.

This job has two different types of challenges: technical problems and people problems. On any project, it takes a while to grasp the technical requirements and come up with solutions. The same goes for the people working on the project. Because you're working with other people, you all need to develop a consensus on what should be done. Although different designs will work, you can choose only one, and people generally have their own preferences, which may not be yours.

WHAT YOU SHOULD KNOW:
Summer work within the field is very beneficial. It allows you to see what's going on in a corporation, and gives you a better idea of what kind of electives to take in college. Also, if you can take courses or get any kind of exposure to the field in high school, it's a good idea. When I was hired, four or five years ago, most of the people in my area were coming in with electrical engineering degrees. Now, however, there's more concentration in computer science.

To do this job, you need to be flexible. You need to be able to juggle different projects, and to be willing to work long hours. A typical week runs about ten hours longer than the usual nine-to-five job. And when there are problems, weeks can be more than sixty hours long. Sometimes you have to come in early in the morning and stay late into the night.

Someone coming in with a master's degree in science would probably start out at around $40,000. Then, typically, that kind of person would soon move into a management position in the engineering arena and make even more money.

Cheryl works to make old telephone company circuit boards more efficient.

"Being a good teacher is like being a good coach. It takes patience and confidence."

WALTER PRUE

ROBOTICS INSTRUCTOR

San Jose, California

WHAT I DO:
I work for a company that makes industrial robots, and I teach our customers how to use and maintain them. Although most of my work is done at our facility in San Jose, I spend about one week in every eight teaching on-site at a customer's location.

The most common function our robots perform is something called "pick and place." Often in manufacturing plants things need to be taken off assembly lines and put in different places. A robot can do this very accurately and often much faster than a human being can. Robots are also well suited to other tasks requiring high speed and good vision. For example, they can be used to install components onto circuit boards and to inspect transistors.

Walter shows a customer how to operate an industrial robot.

The courses we give include a user's course, a programming course, a vision course, and a maintenance course. In the user's course, we teach people how to operate the robots. The programming course teaches technicians how to program the robots so that they can do their tasks, and it's the course I'm most involved with. The vision course is really an advanced programming course that covers the placement and calibration of the cameras that the robot uses to see. In the maintenance course, we introduce problems into the robot's system so that clients can get hands-on experience correcting them.

In addition to teaching, I spend about a week each month researching, rewriting, and upgrading my materials. In the course of this work, I talk regularly with the engineers and designers

Walter teaches a course on how to program robots.

working on the robots, and they keep me up-to-date on the latest developments.

HOW I GOT STARTED:
I'm not quite sure how I got into this work. When I was in high school, I wanted to be a football player, and I kept playing in college, where I went on a navy scholarship. Eventually, though, I dropped football and concentrated instead on my engineering degree.

My first engineering job was in nuclear power, but that field died down in the middle of the 1980s. Then I worked at a hospital for a while, doing radiation therapy. A little later, I got my first job in robotics. I was working for the federal government as a design engineer, and some of the navy projects I worked on were simulator systems that used robotics.

While I was working on the navy projects, I also taught college classes at night. I liked doing this, and I decided that what I really wanted to do was to teach high school and coach football. Unfortunately, I would have had to go back to school to get a teaching credential. And anyway, I couldn't afford to live on a high school teacher's salary. I took this job instead. I was already qualified for it, and it pays pretty well.

HOW I FEEL ABOUT IT:
All in all, I'm pretty happy. The only improvement I'd make is that I'd prefer to teach at the high-school level because the need is greater there. Here, the students are already highly educated and have good futures ahead of them. In high schools, there are still lots of kids who need encouragement and help.

WHAT YOU SHOULD KNOW:
Not everyone is cut out to be a teacher — a good one, that is. Being a good teacher is like being a good coach. Good coaches believe that by developing individuals they can bring the whole squad up to a certain level. This takes patience and confidence, both in your ability to teach and in your students' ability to learn.

In contrast, a teacher who is impatient with students who can't keep up can really do them harm. These students will lose belief in their ability to learn and become so discouraged that they stop trying to achieve anything for themselves. So, before deciding to become a teacher, you should consider whether you have the right temperament for the job.

Most major companies that make robotics or computers have a branch that provides technical instruction to customers. To get a job in this area, it's necessary to have enough of a technical background so that you can learn to teach the courses. Here, we spend four weeks giving new instructors the specific knowledge they need.

Although I teach from 8:30 to 4:00, the hours are more like 7:00 to 7:00 because I need to spend time making sure the demonstration robots will do what I expect them to do. The salary ranges from $35,000 to $50,000.

Walter consults with a student programmer.

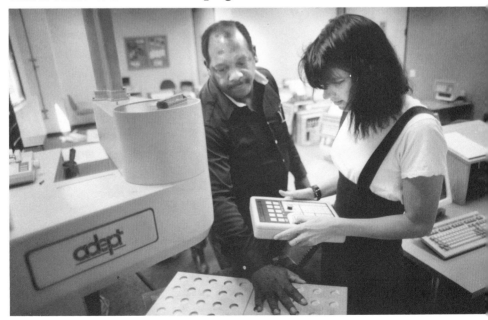

25

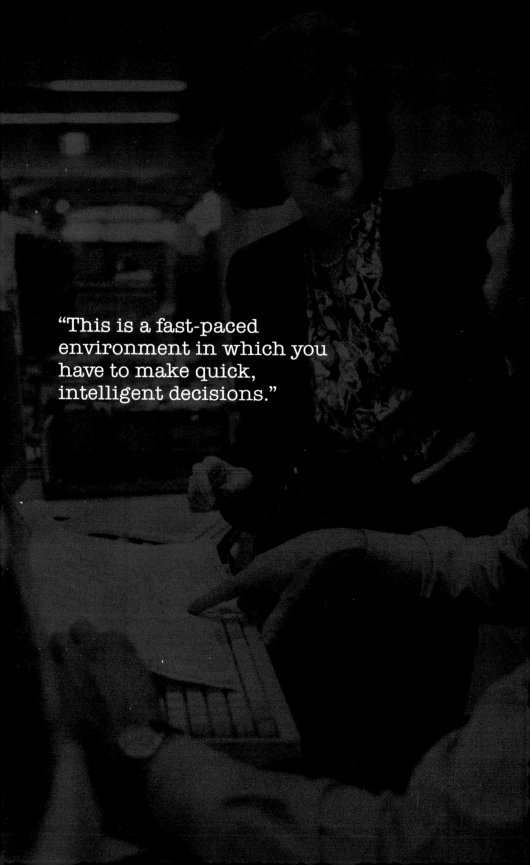

"This is a fast-paced environment in which you have to make quick, intelligent decisions."

WENDY PEREZ

HARDWARE RESEARCHER

New York, New York

WHAT I DO:

I'm a project leader at PC Labs, which is part of the personal computer monthly *PC Magazine*. PC Labs collaborates with the editorial department of *PC Magazine* to produce the magazine's hardware features. Specifically, we provide technical knowledge and test all the new hardware products. The editorial staff takes what we've found and incorporates it into articles.

Most of my time is spent with personal computers. When my team researches PCs, we look at every aspect of that piece of hardware — its speed, the quality of its construction, its documentation, and the level of company support.

A typical project cycle runs about six months. When the machines arrive, the first

thing we do is "benchmark" them. This means that our own technical support group tests the machines to show how well they stand up to certain benchmark performance measures developed by *PC Magazine*. When the results of these tests are in, I look them over and create a "feature script," which is a list of questions about the computer's components. Then I give the machines and the script to freelance reviewers who open up the machines, check them out, and fill in a script for each of them.

When the scripts come back, I process the technical information and write up an explanation of it, which I give to the editorial staff, with the reviewer's work, to turn into a feature. Then, after the feature is completed, I do a technical read to verify that the diagrams, facts, and technical details are accurate.

Wendy develops technical information for articles.

Wendy discusses a feature with one of the writers.

HOW I GOT STARTED:

I've always been very number-oriented and interested in logic. In a way, math and logic led me to computers because computer work requires a lot of problem solving and deduction.

In college, I majored in statistics, and I also did some computer programming on a mainframe, which is a very large and powerful computer. Then a large bank hired me to work in data processing. I went through a training program and learned about computer networking and telecommunications. Much of my work involved the bank's mainframe, but I also learned a lot about PCs.

While I was at the bank, I found that I didn't like mainframe work, so I left and took a six-month job setting up a computer network at an insurance company. It was new to me, fun to learn, and gave me the experience I needed for my next job at an investment bank. After the investment bank, I came here. Although the job was a bit above my skills, I'm quick and I love to learn. I told this to *PC Magazine*, and they hired me.

HOW I FEEL ABOUT IT:

This is a great job. It's a fast-paced environment in which you have to make quick, intelligent decisions. Because we don't have a lot of corporate levels, everyone has the chance to learn, to take on responsibility, and to grow just about as quickly as they can. As a result, we're excited about what we do, take pride in our work, and have made this the top magazine in the industry.

The hours, however, are long and hard, and you can't get away from the office for long. I work from 9:00 A.M. to at least 7:00 P.M., and often much longer. When I'm traveling, I call in constantly to check on things. Sometimes, when I'm very pressured, I dream about the job.

WHAT YOU SHOULD KNOW:
To work in the computer industry, you need to be willing to keep up with new developments. For product testing in particular, you need good communications and writing skills because you're doing so much explaining and interpreting. You also have to be able to handle a fast-paced environment and work independently.

The pay is very rewarding, however. In the labs, the pay is on the computer industry scale rather than the publishing scale. A project manager can make over $45,000, and the director of the labs makes more. In addition, this work prepares you for other jobs. After working here, you can evaluate products for a corporation or become a freelance PC reviewer. Experienced PC reviewers can write up to ten reviews in a week, and at $500 a review, it adds up.

Wendy tests new hardware for speed and quality.

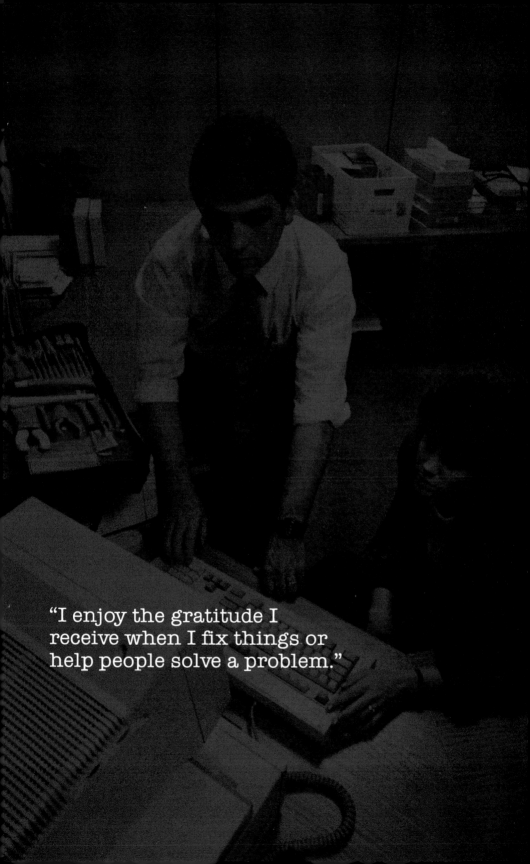

"I enjoy the gratitude I receive when I fix things or help people solve a problem."

RICK WOOD

COMPUTER REPAIRMAN

Pittsfield, Massachusetts

WHAT I DO:
I work for a computer retailer that offers a repair service to its major accounts. Some clients buy a service contract for specific machines. If something goes wrong with one of them, a service technician is dispatched. But we also offer an on-site service program that provides for a full-time technician at the client's location.

On-site work is what I do, and my account is a major corporation. I'm responsible for the daily operation of more than a thousand computers in five locations in two states. I repair all the broken equipment and install all the new and rented equipment.

On a typical day, I show up at my central office at one of the corporation's locations and answer my calls, checking

Rick performs on-site repair for one of his customers.

on the trouble and correcting the problems by phone if I can. After that, I make my rounds to the other locations. I go to the four Pittsfield offices every day, but the New York State office is too far away to visit more than twice a week.

I also maintain an inventory of about $200,000 in parts at my central office. During the day, parts come in — sometimes for computers that are down, sometimes just for stock — and I log them into a data base that I've created. When I send out parts, I log them out.

HOW I GOT STARTED:
When I was in high school, I took a course in computers. I didn't retain much of it, but that was the beginning of my interest. Personal computers were just coming out, and I bought a home model, although it was just for the games I could play on it.

Rick installs a new corporate computer system.

I went to college for a year and studied electronic engineering, but then I left school to work as an electronics technician. I tested the circuitry used in submarines and other defense equipment, and while I was doing this, I noticed how important computers were becoming in all sorts of fields. Even our test equipment was computerized. So I learned as much as I could about computers and went back to school at night to learn even more. After a while, production slowed down and I was forced to take a layoff. But then I found this job.

HOW I FEEL ABOUT IT:
I like working with both people and computers. I enjoy the gratitude I receive when I fix things or help people solve a problem. It's great to be complimented on my efficiency and to see how the results of my work help people. I also like learning about computers, and the fact that my employer provides continuing education and training programs is one of the many good things about the company.

The only negative thing about this job is that the work load can get too heavy. However, I receive a lot of support. My boss stays in touch with me, and other technical people are available if I need them.

WHAT YOU SHOULD KNOW:
I would suggest getting involved with computers as early as possible — at the junior high or high school level, if you can. Then, if it turns out you like them, and you become interested in computer programming or repair, there are a number of routes you can take. There are a lot of good two-year degree programs in electronics and computer repair work. These programs give you a lot of hands-on experience and teach you everything you need to know about the circuitry that makes each component work.

People with two-year degrees can start in repair jobs that pay $18,000 to $25,000. Later, with experience, you can move into positions that pay a little more. At my company, for example, you can get involved in setting up computer networks, and that pays between $35,000 and $50,000. Beyond that, some people end up going into management. In fact, my manager once held a position similar to mine.

Rick's work requires a lot of technical training.

"I like the speed of development. I can create a small-scale model of an idea in a day."

HOWARD YELLEN

SOFTWARE DEVELOPER

Berkeley, California

WHAT I DO:

I'm a partner in a company that develops and markets legal software. Right now, we have two products on the market: a legal research program, and an educational program that prepares law school graduates for the bar exam. We're also developing new products, and we're especially interested in applying the structure of the bar review program to other standardized tests. All of our products are designed to be sold to the public.

Because we're a small company — only six employees altogether — my partner and I do a lot of different things. We try to come up with products that don't create complicated technical problems. We also look for markets of users who have specific interests and are easy to

Howard develops and markets software for legal research.

reach. When we find a good combination, we take our idea to the programmers.

Once we sit down with the programmers, the interaction that develops a usable program begins. On one end is a programmer. He knows computers and has the technical expertise. On the other end is my partner, who has relatively little technical knowledge. He plays the part of the user and talks about the things that confuse him or why he thinks a particular program won't work.

I sit in the middle. I have some technical knowledge, but I can still see things from the point of view of the user. We probably spend about 25 percent of our time trying to figure out how to make our programs easier to use.

HOW I GOT STARTED:

When I graduated from college in 1982, personal computers had just come out.

They were extremely expensive and not very powerful. In Japan, however, where I moved in 1983, computers were all over. I bought one, but it was just a hobby then and had nothing to do with the work that I did.

I came back from Japan in 1984 and began doing data base programming for a small company in New Jersey. Then I got a job with a computer company in Atlanta, where I learned how to repair computers and provide technical support to users. I did that for a couple of years until I went to law school. But even there I continued to work with computers. I was the computer systems manager for the school, and this helped pay my tuition.

It was at law school that I first came up with the idea for the legal research program. I thought there was a need for it, and a friend of mine agreed. We created a prototype, developed a business plan, found investors, and formed a company. At first we used an outside programming company to develop the software, but now we have our own programmers on staff.

HOW I FEEL ABOUT IT:
I like the fact that we're a small company, because I get to wear a lot of hats. I think

Howard discusses a program with his partner.

Howard works out some bugs with the programmers.

like a developer, a programmer, and a user. I also like the speed of development. When I have an idea, I can create a small-scale model of it in a day. Then, once other people react to the model, we can create the actual software very quickly.

WHAT YOU SHOULD KNOW:
There are many different ways to get into software development. You can come to it from a technical background, as our programmers do. Or you can be an informed user, like my partner or myself. The key, however, especially if you're non-technical, is to be creative and observant. Our first product came from my own experience with legal research. But now I read all sorts of magazines from different industries, such as *Travel Agent Today*, to get ideas about programs that might be useful.

There's a huge potential in starting your own business, both for financial rewards and for personal fulfillment. If our products take off, we'll all get rich. And that includes our employees, because we've given them shares in the company. We'll also have the satisfaction of having shaped something and grown with it. We will have taken our ideas and turned them into useful products that make life easier for people.

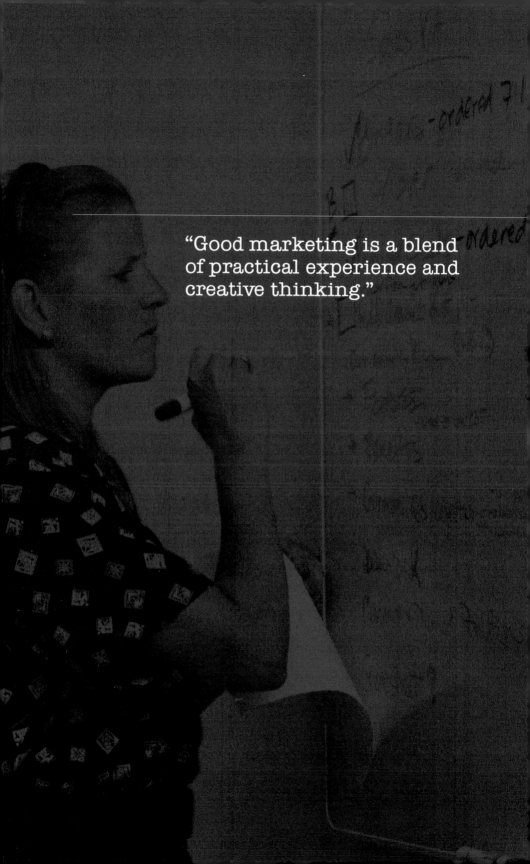

"Good marketing is a blend of practical experience and creative thinking."

MARY ALICE LILIEHOLM

SOFTWARE MARKETER

Redwood Shores, California

WHAT I DO:
The software company I work for produces relational data base management systems. These are data base programs that keep track of information about such things as employees, prices, sales, and so on. I'm responsible for marketing a series of computer-based products that train people to use our products. Data base programs are useful because once the information is in the data base, it becomes very easy to manipulate. For instance, you could look up one particular product and find out every customer who has purchased that product. Or you could look up a customer and find a list of every product that customer has bought.

Data bases are complicated, though, and there's a lot to learn if you want to use

Mary Alice makes up sales kits to market software products.

them well. The courses I market — packages of computer disks and books — meet this need. One course explains what a data base is. Another shows users how to build data bases. We also have courses that teach people SQL, a computer language often used to access data bases.

As product marketing manager for these courses, I talk to customers and determine their needs and preferences. Then I analyze this research and determine the kinds of products people might need. Finally, I give this information to the technical people who create the new products. Once the products are developed, I'm involved in marketing them through advertising, public relations, trade shows, and direct mail.

HOW I GOT STARTED:
When I was in college, I pursued the subjects that

Mary Alice's research helps develop new products.

most interested me — English and theater. But I didn't make a career in either one of these areas because I thought they were too unpredictable. Instead, I became a teacher.

Unfortunately, though I liked teaching, the salaries were low and there weren't many jobs. I became a sales representative for a publisher of college textbooks, but after selling for a while, I realized that sales wasn't for me.

Although I was a good communicator, I wasn't motivated enough. I couldn't get myself to stay on campus that extra hour to make that extra sale. But being in sales taught me enough about marketing to know that I was interested in it.

Around that time, I met a woman who was just starting up a small company that produced videos teaching people how to use personal computers. She needed a marketing person, and I went to work for her. She was a great manager, teacher, and mentor. And because the company was small, I had the opportunity to learn a lot.

HOW I FEEL ABOUT IT:
Now I work in a small division of a large company. This gives me the best of both worlds. In large companies, marketing is often split into separate jobs — research, operations, analysis, and communications. But when you're in a small company, or a small division within a large company, you get to perform all these tasks yourself. However, because the company itself is large, I can draw on greater resources than a small company could provide.

Another thing I like about this work is that it's basically problem solving. I enjoy identifying a problem and then solving it. It's fun. I sit down and come up with every possible solution, from the most minimal to the most extravagant. Then I consider even more absurd possibilities, because embedded in the absurd there may be the beginning of a practical idea.

WHAT YOU SHOULD KNOW: There are different ways to get into this field. In small companies, you can still get into marketing without a graduate degree. Large companies, however, tend to restrict their hiring to people with M.B.A. degrees. These degrees have become rubber stamps. They don't necessarily help you on the job, but they keep you from being weeded out during hiring.

Good marketing is a blend of practical experience and creative thinking. What I learned in school — reading and comparing different authors' work — may not sound like marketing. But in fact, whether you're writing an English paper or doing market research, you look at a problem and decide how to tackle it by comparing one situation to another.

The pay in marketing depends on your background and experience. Entry-level positions pay in the $20,000 range. But when you've moved up to the middle-management levels, you can earn between $40,000 and $60,000. Marketing jobs top out somewhere in the low six-figure range.

Mary Alice promotes new software at a trade show.

"I like seeing students'
minds expand as they grasp
and use new concepts."

ANDREA LAWRENCE

COMPUTER SCIENCE PROFESSOR

Atlanta, Georgia

WHAT I DO:

I teach computer science at Spelman College, a four-year liberal arts college in Atlanta, Georgia. The usual teaching load is four classes per semester, but I teach only three because I also direct the computer science program, and there's a lot of administrative work involved with that.

During a typical semester, I'll teach classes on such subjects as programming in the Pascal language; artificial intelligence; and computer literacy, which is a course that familiarizes social science and humanities majors with the computer. Altogether, I spend nine or ten hours a week in the classroom and another six to eight hours holding formal office hours, during which time students can come and talk to me. But I have so much else to do on campus that I'm usually here at least forty hours each week.

Much of this extra time is spent attending to my advisory and administrative responsibilities. I serve as an academic advisor to all of the seniors in the department, and I also advise a selection of other students, especially those with special needs such as transfer students. My administrative duties include working on the departmental budget, writing grant proposals, supervising textbook selection, and developing new courses.

HOW I GOT STARTED:

Math was one of my interests as a child, and my grandmother, who was an elementary school teacher, strongly encouraged me. By the time I began thinking about college, I knew that I would major in math.

Andrea talks to a student from her computer literacy class.

43

After I got my B.S. in math, I spent some time raising a family. Then I began teaching at a high school, and there I began to get a lot of exposure to computers. When I studied math in college, computer science was not at all widely taught or applied. But by the time I was teaching high school, between 1978 and 1983, computers had become much more common in the classroom, and I used them to teach mathematics. I also took some courses myself in computer science, and became interested enough to pursue a master's degree in the field.

While I was getting my master's degree at Atlanta University, I was assigned to a teaching assistant's position at Spelman. At that time, I discovered that I enjoyed teaching in a college setting. So when I got my master's degree, I applied for and got a position here. Now I'm working on my Ph.D., which is a degree that you need to stay in college teaching for the long term.

HOW I FEEL ABOUT IT:
I like seeing students' minds expand as they grasp and use new concepts. No matter what I was teaching, I would have that satisfaction. But I'm especially pleased to be teaching them something as useful as computer science. Once students get a computer science degree, they're able to get good jobs or go on to graduate school.

Andrea directs Spelman's computer science program.

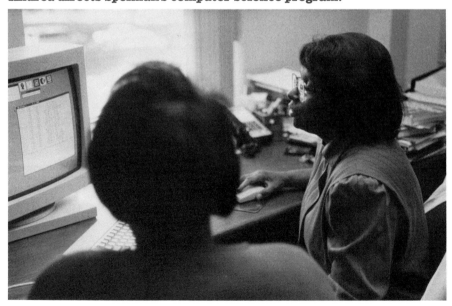

Andrea teaches three classes each semester.

Teaching is very important to me. Although I've often thought that I might like to get into software design, I think that teaching is where I can make the greatest contribution. As a black woman in a technical field, I feel that I provide a positive role model for the students in my class, a model that could not be easily replaced were I to leave.

WHAT YOU SHOULD KNOW:
If you're interested in teaching computer science, get involved with computers at as early an age as you can.

Take whatever computer courses are offered in your junior high school and high school, and try to get a good science and math background. Also, when you're choosing a college, choose carefully. Make sure that it offers the kind of courses you want, and that its students will be ones you'll feel comfortable with.

The pay can range from very low to very high depending on the size of the university and whether it's public or private. The entry-level range is anywhere from the mid-$20,000 range to nearly $50,000.

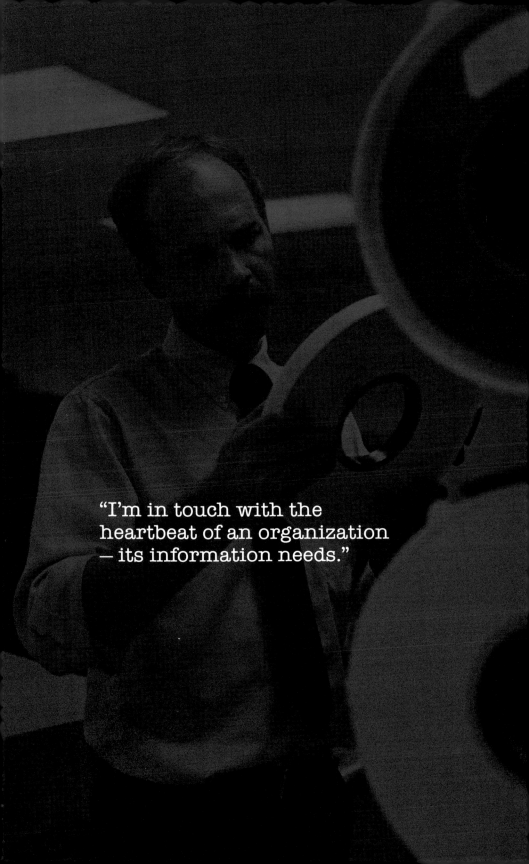

"I'm in touch with the
heartbeat of an organization
— its information needs."

DAN BOUTILIER

DATA MANAGER

Portland, Maine

WHAT I DO:
I manage all the data processing needs of the Portland city government. My staff of thirteen, which includes eight programmers, provides a wide range of services. Some you might expect, such as keeping track of the city's financial records. But we also keep track of marriage certificates, death certificates, and business licenses. And we're heavily involved with public safety.

The police's 911 emergency number is tied into a computer dispatching network, and we write the program code that makes it work. We also provide programming support for police and fire department recordkeeping. We record data on each fire call, for example, noting things like the number of trucks and firefighters that responded and the number of feet of fire hose used to fight the fire.

In order to do our job well, we need to examine the computer needs of each department of the city government. We begin by meeting with departmental representatives, who discuss their problems with us. Then we collect samples of the data that's involved, and my programmers develop software to manage it. I monitor things and solve some of the technical problems that come up. I also meet with the end users (the people who use the software) in the various departments to report on the progress we're making and to make sure there have been no additional developments that would change the shape of the program.

HOW I GOT STARTED:
I got into this field when I was just 16 years old. My

Dan manages all the computer data for the city of Portland.

Dan's office keeps records for the fire department.

high school offered juniors and seniors a two-year vocational program in computer training. Because I liked computers and solving problems, I went into the program.

When I graduated from high school in the early 1970s, computers were expensive. Large businesses could afford state-of-the-art equipment, but most colleges couldn't. So I went straight into business. I took a job and in four years worked my way up from computer operator to programmer. I also took advantage of all the training courses the company offered, and I taught myself what I needed to know.

Eventually, I got a job with the city as a programmer. From there, I was made a programmer-analyst, which is a programmer who meets with end users to discuss their needs. Next, I was promoted to systems programmer, the top technical position, and then to the job I have now.

HOW I FEEL ABOUT IT:
When you work in data processing, you're in touch with the heartbeat of an organization — its information needs. You're constantly looking for ways the organization can improve its efficiency and better exploit its computer systems. This can be a very complex and challenging process.

WHAT YOU SHOULD KNOW:
A person who's thinking of this type of work should be a good problem solver, and part of being a good problem solver is being patient. You have to overcome the tendency

to get frustrated when you're confronted with a particularly difficult problem. Fortunately, as you gain more skills and learn more computer languages, it becomes easier to solve problems.

Nowadays, for this type of work, it's a good idea to have at least a two-year associate's degree, and a bachelor of science degree is even better. The courses you take should be a balance between business management and computer science. Someone with this type of background could probably enter a data processing shop at the programmer or programmer-analyst level. Because I entered without a degree, I had to begin in the computer operations area.

The hours are really what you make them. Although this could be a nine-to-five job, I tend to work more than that. When I was first promoted to this position, I worked seventy hours a week because there was a great deal to accomplish in a short period of time. Now, I tend to work from 8:00 A.M. to 6:00 P.M. every day.

The pay in data management depends on the level of your responsibility. In a city government the size of Portland's, the pay range for someone with my level of responsibility is $42,000 to $48,000 a year. In a large corporation or a larger city, however, the pay scale is higher.

Dan solves technical problems when they come up.

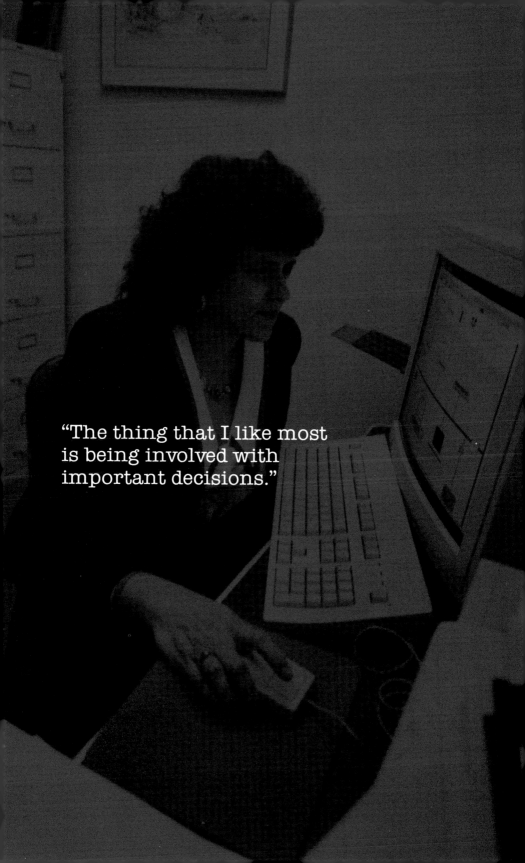

"The thing that I like most is being involved with important decisions."

RUTH HILDENBERGER
SYSTEMS ENGINEER

Alexandria, Virginia

WHAT I DO:

I work for a research and development center that helps the federal government acquire large computer hardware and software systems. For example, the Internal Revenue Service might need a new system to process tax returns. But the accountants and auditors there don't have the expertise to know what they need. So they come to my company for help.

My department works mainly with large acquisitions. When a government agency needs to buy a new software system, we help them write the specifications. In other words, we spell out what's needed. Private companies use these specifications to bid on the job, and we evaluate the proposals that come in. Then,

Ruth helps select computer systems for the government.

after a supplier is selected, we follow up and make sure that the final product fits the specifications and quality standards outlined in the bid.

Although we don't write the actual software that will be used, we often develop small models of what's needed. To do this, we'll interview the potential users, determine their needs, and come up with a little personal computer version of something that might be useful. We show this prototype to the users, get their comments, and revise the prototype until it's what they want. Then outside companies examine this product and use it to help them bid.

HOW I GOT STARTED:

My father was a manufacturing manager at General Electric for over thirty years, and he saw the computer revolution coming. He told me that I should learn to program computers. I never would have thought of it on my own. But I took my father's advice and got a two-year associate's degree in data processing technology.

After I got my degree, I went to Washington to get a job as a programmer. Unfortunately, the only job I could get was as a data entry clerk. Although I did get a programming job three months later, I realized that I had to continue my education. So for the next five years, I went to school part-time and eventually got a B.S. in information systems.

Once I got my B.S., I moved around a bit. I followed up my B.S. with a master's degree in information science. Then I gave up my full-time job to have a child and work from my home instead, helping small businesses select and set up personal computer systems. When I was ready to come back to work full time, I got a job where I am right now.

HOW I FEEL ABOUT IT:

The thing I like most about this work is being involved with important decisions. In the last three years, I've been in on at least twenty meetings in which policy decisions involving millions of dollars were made. Although I don't make the decisions myself, I am asked questions about the software that's involved, so my knowledge and opinions have an impact on what's going on.

Another good thing about my work is its variety. We

Ruth presents information about a new system.

Ruth outlines a program for the Agriculture Department.

change clients at least once every six months, and we're often working with more than one client at a time. For example, now I'm working on projects both for the Bureau of Land Management and for the Department of Agriculture. In a few months, I could be working for the F.B.I. or the State Department. There are always different situations and problems to consider.

WHAT YOU SHOULD KNOW:
In terms of schooling, there are two basic choices: You can go into either computer science or information systems. Computer science is primarily concerned with developing software for scientific applications. That's the department for the physicists and engineers. In information systems, however, computer science concepts are applied to financial, governmental, and other administrative problems. As you study, you should decide whether you're a scientist or an applications person, and choose your major accordingly.

The hours are pretty consistently 7:45 A.M. to 5:00 P.M. However, there are exceptions when deadlines are near. Then you work nights and weekends to finish up. Also, if you're obsessed with being promoted, you've got to attend conferences, publish papers, and put in long hours.

The pay is good. I make $45,000, which is more than I ever thought I would. At the upper levels, obviously, there's the potential for much higher salaries.

"We take some problem that people solve all the time and determine exactly how people solve it."

MARK KRIEGSMAN

KNOWLEDGE ENGINEER

Boston, Massachusetts

WHAT I DO:
I work for a company that specializes in knowledge engineering, or artificial intelligence. In knowledge engineering, we take some problem that people solve all the time, and determine exactly how people solve it — what knowledge and rules they use to solve it. Then we break down those rules and translate them into a program code that a computer can apply.

Most of our work involves business or financial applications. For example, a bank may come to us because they want a program that tells them whether or not to approve a loan. We'll start work on such a program by asking the bank's loan officers how they go about approving loans. We'll also look at case histories of loans that were approved and rejected. From all this information, we'll develop an outline of the procedure typically used by the bank to make loan decisions. And then we'll turn that human procedure into software code so that the computer can replicate a loan officer's behavior.

After the program is delivered to the client, there's usually a six-month to one-year period during which the client points out factors the program isn't taking into account, as well as other problems. Periodically, we'll go back into the program and correct these errors by changing the decision-making rules.

HOW I GOT STARTED:
In high school, I developed a strong interest in computers, philosophy, and language. Then, as I became further involved with them, it seemed to me that the place they

Mark programs computers to think the way people do.

all met was in artificial intelligence, because artificial intelligence is the area of computer science that most nearly approximates the human mind.

Although I used computers in high school, I didn't do much formal study of them until much later. Instead, I fooled around with them on my own. I did things like work in a local computer shop and create and publish my own video game. By the time I got to college, I already knew a lot about computers, so I studied cognitive science instead. Cognitive science is a four-way blend of psychology, computer science, philosophy, and linguistics. It's essentially the study of the human mind and how it works, and it prepared me for the job I have now, which I got right out of college.

HOW I FEEL ABOUT IT:
We get a wide variety of projects, most of which are very interesting. For example, I'm working on a program now that will write business letters in different languages. The problem is more challenging than it seems because the program needs to respond to cultural differences. For instance, while we might say "I appreciate this opportunity to be of service," the French equivalent might be something that, literally translated, means "If there's ever anything I can do for you, I am always your servant." If the software didn't respond to this, there might be misunderstandings.

Mark tailors programs to meet his clients' needs.

Mark programs computers to do jobs done by people.

The environment here is also good. Because everyone who works here has to be interdisciplinary, they're a creative bunch. The atmosphere is relaxed and the hours are flexible. It's just the kind of place you need to solve problems. Although there are schedules to be met, the deadlines are mixed. Some are long-term and some are day-to-day.

WHAT YOU SHOULD KNOW:
Artificial intelligence work requires enough programming skills that you don't have to stop and think about the programming language you're using. Beyond that, what's helpful is any degree that involves the study of the human mind. This includes psychology, sociology, philos-ophy, linguistics, and the study of foreign languages.

The pay is excellent. Entry-level salaries range from $30,000 to $40,000 a year, and there's the potential to move up quickly. Eventually, a lot of people start their own companies and do consulting work. The earning potential in consulting is especially high – as much as $1500 a day.

The hours are completely random. A day's work can be six hours or twelve hours, whatever it takes to get the job done. The worst stretch I've had was the time I worked from 8:00 A.M. Sunday until 10:00 P.M. Monday without a break. We had to ship a product by Tuesday in order to get paid, so there wasn't any choice.

"I've worked on everything from airplane simulators to machines that simulate space flight."

DON SMALL

FLIGHT SIMULATOR

Houston, Texas

WHAT I DO:
Because I've been designing flight simulators for more than thirty-five years, I've worked on everything from airplane simulators to machines that simulate space flight. Right now, I'm working on a simulator for a space station.

To understand my work, you have to understand what a flight simulator is. A simulator's function is to prepare pilots, crew members, and astronauts for flight. When we design a simulator, we create a machine that will replicate the trainee's future environment as closely as possible. The trainee uses the same controls found in the actual vehicle.

HOW I GOT STARTED:
I didn't start by pursuing a career in flight simulation.

Don designs a simulator to prepare astronauts for flight.

When I went to college, I began as a pre-med student. But I didn't like that side of science, so I moved into electronics.

After college, I got a job with a flight simulation company called Link. Link was just switching over from mechanical air trainers to electronic trainers, and they were recruiting electronics people like myself. I started as a field engineer, working in the factory to gain an understanding of the equipment. Then I went to the customers, trained them to use the equipment, and made any modifications that were necessary.

After that, I became involved with the space program. I worked on the Gemini mission simulator and other space flight simulators until 1969, when I moved to Houston to work with NASA on the Apollo program. After Apollo ended, I headed teams

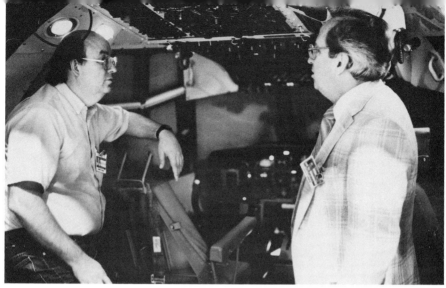

Don stands in the cockpit of an airplane simulator.

that built the simulator for the space shuttle.

HOW I FEEL ABOUT IT:

What's challenging about this work is that it explores every branch of science there is. We have to model the behavior of the real world so that what a person feels is exactly coordinated with what he or she hears and sees. That means really getting into a person's senses. To do this, you need a variety of engineering skills, and you must constantly call on all of your training and experience.

WHAT YOU SHOULD KNOW:

Today, most of the people we hire have computer science, electrical engineering, or physics degrees. Some even have simulation-related degrees. But even if you get one of these degrees, you still have to be trained as a sys-

tems engineer by Link or one of its competitors.

Normally, this is a regular eight-to-five job. However, there are times when you'll be working over sixty hours a week. This tends to occur either in the development cycle when things don't go as planned, or later during the space mission itself when something that wasn't anticipated happens. When I was working on Apollo 13, for example, one of the ship's tanks exploded on the way to the moon. I was part of a team that helped figure out a way to get the crew back before its supplies were exhausted. On that mission, I worked for thirty-six hours straight.

Starting pay in this field is better than average for people in the sciences, and senior staff positions reach the $80,000 range.

Related Careers

Here are more computer-related careers you may want to explore:

ANIMATOR
Animators use computers to generate images, which are then filmed to produce cartoons and other animation.

COMPUTER SECURITY CONSULTANT
Computer security consultants specialize in protecting computer networks and data bases from unauthorized access and tampering.

COMPUTER SERVICE REPRESENTATIVE
Computer service representatives work at companies that rent out time on computer terminals and print files from customers' computer disks.

DATA ENTRY CLERK
Data entry clerks work for large companies and governmental agencies entering information into data base programs.

DOCUMENTATION WRITER
Documentation writers create the manuals that explain how computers and computer programs work so that non-professionals can understand how to use them.

ELECTRICAL ENGINEER
Electrical engineers design electronic equipment such as computers, stereos, and radar.

GRAPHIC DESIGNER
Graphic designers use computers to create illustrations and layouts for advertisements, magazines, pamphlets, and books.

METEOROLOGIST
Meteorologists study the atmosphere. Using computers, they analyze this information in order to understand the climate and predict the weather.

OPINION RESEARCHER
Opinion researchers use polls and surveys to gather information on people's views, which they then organize and analyze using computers.

SEISMOLOGIST
Seismologists study the vibrations and plate movements of the earth so that they can predict earthquakes.

SOFTWARE TRAINER
Software trainers offer personalized instruction in the operation of specific computer programs.

TYPESETTER
Typesetters use computer programs and equipment to set type and do page layouts for books and magazines.

Organizations

Contact these organizations for information about the following careers:

KNOWLEDGE ENGINEER
American Association for Artificial Intelligence
445 Burgess Drive, Menlo Park, CA 94025

DATA MANAGER
American Federation of Information Processing Societies
1815 North Lynn Street, Suite 800, Arlington, VA 22209

FLIGHT SIMULATOR
American Institute of Aeronautics and Astronautics
1290 Avenue of the Americas, New York, NY 10104

COMMUNICATIONS ENGINEER
American Institute of Industrial Engineers
25 Technology Park/Atlanta, Norcross, GA 30092

SYSTEMS ENGINEER
Association for Systems Management
24587 Baghy Road, Cleveland, OH 44138

COMPUTER SCIENCE
Association for Women in Computing
10701 Green Mountain Circle, Columbia, MD 21044

PROGRAMMER
Association of Computer Programmers and Analysts
11800 Sunrise Valley Drive, Suite 808, Reston, VA 22091

DATA MANAGER
Data Processing Management Association
550 Busse Highway, Park Ridge, IL 60068

SYSTEMS ENGINEER
Independent Computer Consultants Association
Box 27412, St. Louis, MO 63141

ROBOTICS INSTRUCTOR
International Robotics
611 Broadway, Suite 422-A, New York, NY 10012

ROBOTICS INSTRUCTOR
Robotics Institute of America
One SME Drive, P.O. Box 1366, Dearborn, MI 48121

FLIGHT SIMULATOR
Society for Computer Simulation
P.O. Box 2228, La Jolla, CA 94038

Books

CAREER CHOICES FOR STUDENTS OF COMPUTER SCIENCE
New York: Walker & Co., 1985.

CAREERS IN COMPUTERS
By Lila B. Stair. Lincolnwood, Ill.: National Textbook Co., 1988.

CAREERS IN COMPUTERS: THE HIGH-TECH JOB GUIDE
By Texe W. Marrs. New York: Monarch Press, 1984.

CAREERS WITH ROBOTS
By Texe W. Marrs. New York: Facts on File, 1988.

THE COMPLETE AVIATION-AEROSPACE CAREER GUIDE
By Robert Caldrone. Blue Ridge Summit, Pa.: Aero/Tab Books, 1989.

EXPLORING CAREERS IN COMPUTER GRAPHICS
By Richard Masterson. New York: Rosen Publishing, 1987.

EXPLORING CAREERS IN COMPUTER SOFTWARE
By Dorothy Brockman. New York: Rosen Publishing, 1985.

HOW TO BECOME A SUCCESSFUL COMPUTER CONSULTANT
By Alan Simon. New York: McGraw-Hill, 1985.

INFOPRENEURS: TURNING DATA INTO DOLLARS
By H. Skip Weitzen. New York: John Wiley, 1988.

JOBS FOR THE 21ST CENTURY
By Robert V. Weinstein. New York: Collier Books, 1983.

OPPORTUNITIES IN COMPUTER AIDED DESIGN AND COMPUTER AIDED MANUFACTURE
By Jan Bone. Lincolnwood, Ill.: National Textbook Co., 1986.

OPPORTUNITIES IN COMPUTER MAINTENANCE CAREERS
By Elliot S. Kanter. Lincolnwood, Ill.: National Textbook Co., 1988.

THE PROGRAMMER'S SURVIVAL GUIDE: CAREER STRATEGIES FOR COMPUTER PROFESSIONALS
By Janet Ruhl. Englewood Cliffs, N.J.: Yourdon Press, 1989.

THE ROBOTICS CAREERS HANDBOOK
By Ann Cardoza and Suzee J. Vlk. New York: Arco Publishing, 1985.

Glossary Index

004
KAP
    Kaplan, Andrew
        Careers for computer buffs

DATE DUE	BORROWER'S NAME	

004
KAP
    Kaplan, Andrew
        Careers for computer buffs